# GOLD CITIES

## GRASS VALLEY AND NEVADA CITY

Being a history and guide to the ad-
venturesome past of two picturesque
cities of the California gold country

*Photographically conceived and recorded by the sensitive lens of*

## JIM MORLEY

*Assisted in research and text preparation
by historian and long-time resident*

## DORIS FOLEY

HOWELL-NORTH BOOKS · BERKELEY, CALIFORNIA · 1965

## GOLD CITIES — GRASS VALLEY AND NEVADA CITY

*Printed and bound in the United States of America.*
Library of Congress Catalog Card No. 65-18741

Published by Howell-North Books
1050 Parker Street, Berkeley, California 94710

## A Note on this Guide and the Northern Mines

This book is an attempt to portray the fascinating past of Grass Valley and Nevada City mainly through scenes that still exist today, together with stories about those scenes. In a larger sense it is a last long look at a life and time now vanishing.

Insofar as possible, fact has been sifted from the inevitable myths, but even the best sources are occasionally in conflict. Present-day place names have been retained throughout to avoid confusion: Nevada City, for instance, instead of the early name Nevada. Each subject is keyed to its proper map location by a corresponding number in parentheses at the end of the article or caption. Subjects are arranged in an order of going hopefully designed to be convenient and interesting.

These towns are in the Northern Mines, not the Mother Lode. Coloma, El Dorado County, site of James Marshall's discovery of gold January 24, 1848, early was regarded as the approximate dividing point between southern and northern gold fields. Later, quartz miners found a system of ore veins they called the Mother Lode running rope-like up through the Southern Mines and ending near Georgetown, close to Coloma. So the division remains, leaving the Northern Mines a distinct entity having as its heart the towns pictured here.

Our historical heritage is being diminished rapidly by man-made changes and by assaults of time and the elements. May you enjoy these glimpses of an adventurous age.

## Acknowledgments

Gratitude is expressed to all those who assisted in various capacities in the preparation of this guide. Especially helpful were Vivian Berggren, Mrs. E. F. Buck, William Carman, Beatrice Cassidy, Lucille Christe, the late H. P. Davis, Mr. and Mrs. Arthur K. Dunlop, Elisabeth Egenhoff of the California Division of Mines and Geology; Savory Ford; Bernice Glasson and Esther McCluskey of the Nevada City Public Library; Ann Griffin; Isabel Hefelfinger, Director, Nevada County Museum; Robert Ingram, Editor, The Union; Janet L. Johnson, for the excellent map linework; Mr. and Mrs. W. W. Kallenberger; Mr. and Mrs. Elza Kilroy; Theodore Kohler, Recorder, Nevada County; Marian Libbey; Virginia Magnussen; P. C. Mann, General Manager, Empire-Star Mines; Prof. S. G. Morley; Richard Nickless, Curator, Nevada County Museum; the late John E. Nettell; Ruth Rector; Gilbert Tennis; Dean Thompson, Nevada City Nugget; Neils C. Tonnesen, for the fine relief shading on the city maps and for his handsome drawings; and Mr. and Mrs. Rick Worth, National Hotel.

Two most useful references were the late Edmund Kinyon's The Northern Mines and W. D. Johnston, Jr.'s USGS Professional Paper 194, The Gold Quartz Veins of Grass Valley. Equally valuable were the resources of Bancroft Library, the California Historical Society, the Nevada County Historical Society and the Society of California Pioneers. Should any contributor inadvertently have been omitted from this listing, the authors extend their apologies and appreciation.

Stark against a stormy sky, these gigantic pumps that once cleared water from depths of Golden Center Mine form a mechanical Stonehenge telling of past glories.

# GRASS VALLEY

Wagon trains that struggled over Donner Pass in the late 1840's and made their way down the rough western slope of the Sierra found Greenhorn Creek a likely place to camp and rest before they continued the bruising journey to the Sacramento Valley. When cattle wandered from this campsite in search of better feed, the emigrants often found them several miles away grazing peacefully in a meadow that came to be known simply as the grassy valley.

In autumn of 1849 two small groups of emigrants decided to linger here. They built crude cabins to protect against oncoming winter and the company from Boston panned for gold along Wolf Creek at the lower end of the valley. A store was opened, the spot acquired the name Boston Ravine, and settlement began. Briefly it bore the title Centerville and then became Grass Valley.

By that time hordes of gold seekers were pouring over the passes and abandoning ships in San Francisco Bay to head for the mountains. These early miners believed all gold originated in streams, a logical result of Marshall's American River discovery and their own limited experience. Little did they realize, as they trudged along the trail, that the very heart of California's gold lay buried beneath them in solid rock.

Then in the fall of 1850 a ledge of gold-bearing quartz was found on Gold Hill. At first a mere curiosity, the stuff aroused the miners' predatory instincts quickly enough and they swarmed over the site. Gold was so plentiful that claims were limited to one hundred square feet as safeguard against the metal becoming demonetized. Over $2,000,000 was taken out within a few feet of the surface.

5

More veins came to light and several primitive stamp mills were operating by 1852. However, most quartz mining ventures of that era proved disastrous failures for want of knowledge of both geological conditions and proper recovery methods. Below the surface the fractured and twisted lodes were easily lost. Thus no mine produced continually; success would be followed by a shutdown, a transfer of ownership and another try. By the late sixties techniques had improved greatly but many mines were petering out or were tied up in lawsuits over claims to the same ledge, and by 1878 Grass Valley had the reputation of being a worked-out, dying camp.

Salvation came from a stabilized Empire Mine and the consolidation of claims throughout the district. Gradually there emerged three major producing areas: the Idaho-Maryland, the North Star and the Empire. From 1900 to 1925 the North Star, managed by James D. Hague and A. D. Foote, and the Empire under George D. Starr's guidance produced most of the gold mined in Nevada County.

In the hundreds of miles of subterranean workings there were shenanigans aplenty as mines picked their neighbors' ore pockets or saved their own pumps by slyly poking drain holes into adjacent tunnels and letting the other fellow take

care of seepage. Highgrading, the smuggling out of almost pure gold, was the perennial pastime of many a miner.

Underground gold is confined to quartz veins an inch to several feet in thickness sandwiched between rock faces called the hanging wall and foot wall. A favorite local story tells of the miner who ordered pie for dessert and found it so thin the top and bottom crusts almost touched. In disgust he called the waitress and complained "You might as well take this back, 'cause the hangin' wall and foot wall's so close together it ain't worth minin' out!"

Many of these men had made the long journey from the tin mines of Cornwall, England to try their fortune in the New World. It was said that every Cornishman needed a helper and always recommended just the man for the job: "My cousin Jack." And that is how Cornish miners became known as Cousin Jacks. Their superstitions befitted their dangerous occupation. They objected to whistling underground in the belief it set up vibrations which might cause a cave-in. It was bad luck to start a new operation on Friday and for a woman to go underground. There were Jabberwocks (gremlins) in the tunnels, along with Tommyknockers, the spirits of dead miners who tapped warnings of impending disaster on the rock walls.

Still remaining are such Cornish traditions as the peppery meat pie called pasty (*pass*-tee) and

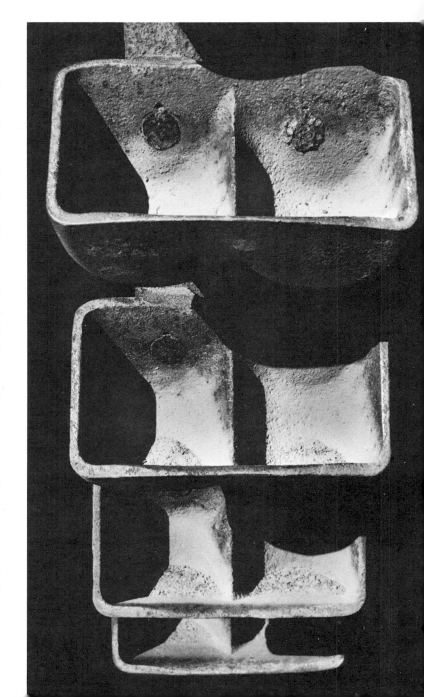

the renowned Cornish Choir. The choir was organized in 1890, although songs floated up from the mine shafts long before that. Every Christmas Eve they assemble on the steps of the Union Building on Mill Street to " 'ave a bit of 'ark 'ark," and crowds gather to hear the fine old music that has been passed from father to son. For years the carols were broadcast to the world from the depths of the Empire.

The mines did a solid business during the Great Depression, then closed temporarily during World War II. Soon thereafter the pumps were pulled permanently as production costs soared above the pegged price for gold. Thus it ended some 100 years after it began, leaving a lot of gold down there yet. Gone is the colorful traffic of the mines, but still left in the piney hills are some of the relics and much of the atmosphere of those famous years, and a climate and location that have brought fresh prosperity to the place where pioneers sought their wandering oxen in those hard, bright days when the West was new.

## Rowe Shaft

In the silent forest a towering headframe rears out of the earth, and from its base a trestle slopes up to ore bins off to the right. This was a secondary and recent approach to the buried treasure of that monarch of mines, the Empire. (1)

# Empire Mines

The oldest, largest and richest mining operation in Grass Valley was that of the Empire, long a magic name. Its main shaft plunged on an incline more than 7000 feet into the earth, reaching a vertical depth of 3500 feet. Miners descended in a skip (car used for hauling men, ore and materials) from the headframe at a speed of 800 feet per minute. By 1928 over $35,000,000 had come out of that shaft, and in all probability this amount has been doubled since.

It all began when George Roberts found the Ophir vein on Ophir Hill in 1850, shortly after the initial discovery of gold-bearing quartz on Gold Hill. Pros-perity followed until 1878, when—crisis!—the mine bottomed at the 1200-foot level, all visible ore exhausted. Three well-known engineers declared the prospects grim.

William B. Bourn Jr., who had just inherited the mine from his father, refused to give up, pressed further exploration, and reaped a bonanza. His baronial mansion, surrounded by formal gardens, was built close to the Empire workings. During Bourn's lifetime it was a showplace and the center of community gatherings. As a wedding gift to his daughter and son-in-law, Bourn presented them with one of

the Lakes of Killarney in Ireland. Today's tourist to
the Emerald Isle may visit the Bourn-Vincent Park
on the shores of the lake purchased with Empire gold.

In 1898 the vein disappeared again, and was found
again; the process repeated in the 1920's. In 1928 the
Empire was acquired by the Newmont Mining Corporation. Rising production costs, culminated by a
strike, forced the mighty Empire to shut down for
good in 1956. Several months were spent cleaning
up gold that had settled into nooks and crannies over
the years. Machinery was sold in 1959 and the mam-
moth stamp mill finally was dismantled, but most of
the structures shown here remain, relics of a robust
century. (2)

At intervals down the main shaft were stations from which drifts (cross tunnels) branched out to reach the ore veins. Miners are eating lunch at the 3400-foot-level station, carved out of solid rock. The figure refers to the number of feet from the surface, measured along the inclined shaft. (Nevada County Historical Society.)

Eventually the carbide lamp replaced the miner's candlestick, and the pneumatic drill did away with hammer and hand drill of song and legend. Drill, blast and muck out was the sequence in stoping, the actual excavation of ore. The stope precisely followed the ore vein, which here appears to be two or three feet thick. Rock above vein is called the hanging wall, rock below vein is footwall. (Nevada County Historical Society.)

Mule power hauled ore and waste rock through the underground maze to the main shaft. Electric locomotives handled the material above ground. (At left, California Division of Mines and Geology.)

In the enveloping dusk, with the pines quiet and the mine manager working late on affairs with a golden past, the Empire office displays all the qualities that make it one of the finest stone structures in the West. Built at the turn of the century, it thus cannot match the mine itself in point of service, but nevertheless blends perfectly with the environs and the historic feeling engendered by the richest workings of them all.

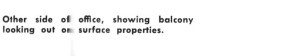

Other side of office, showing balcony looking out on surface properties.

Enclosed catwalk ran from office to mill, allowed manager to check operations and provided secure route to bring gold back to office. This picture was taken during auction of machinery after shutdown.

Deep within the office, in a cave-like room formed of dark, smoky walls arrayed with strange instruments suitable to a medieval torture chamber, the gold finally was melted down and cast into bricks. In this form the metal was shipped to San Francisco for refining and ultimate delivery to the mint, completing the entire process and gladdening the hearts of the mine owners.

Shown above are the two smallest oil-fired furnaces, with a crucible and molds of assorted sizes gathering dust on the floor. Considerable heat was required; gold melts at 2016 degrees Fahrenheit. At left, special tongs gripped the crucible to remove it for pouring.

14

Splendor in the pines: Bourn owned three mansions, one in San Francisco, one on the Peninsula, and this one, designed by Willis Polk and built in the mid-nineties. At right, as seen from the road. Below, the front, viewed across a lotus pond. (3)

Farther down the road is the mine manager's residence with spacious porches well suited to hot summers. Here it is overlaid with the cool shadows of early morning. (4)

15

the plant ceased operations in 1956, except the big wheel (saved by private owner, scrapped in 1939). Now the site is to become a museum. (6)

Above, massive hub is cast iron; the rest is steel. Original buckets were a Risdon Iron Works design of bronze, later replaced by more conventional ones, most of which are missing now. Water at 65 p.s.i. pressure hissed through 1½-inch nozzles to turn wheel. Under these conditions it developed 1000 horsepower. The flywheel effect was enormous.

17

# Pennsylvania

Adjoining the Empire is the Pennsylvania, also once a great producer and in its later years part of the Empire complex. The 4600-foot inclined shaft was equipped with this hoist machinery. Dials calibrated in hundreds of feet showed the levels at which the skip stopped. Thus 46 stands for the 4600-foot level (about 1900 vertical feet down) which was the bottom of the shaft. There it was met by a crosscut tunnel from the Empire. Other corridors connected with the WYOD (Work Your Own Diggings) Mine and some extended as far as Main Street.

It was not unusual for a Grass Valley miner visiting San Francisco to ask the elevator operator to let him off at the 600 level, instead of sixth floor. (5)

# North

Just below the old settlement of Boston Ravine, on the banks of Wolf Creek, stands this monster Pelton wheel in the ruins of an air compressor plant built in 1895. The North Star Mine was preparing to sink the Central Shaft, and power was needed to run its machinery. Since electrical systems of the period were not considered reliable, air was chosen, and water power was to compress the air.

First an 18½-foot diameter wheel was used, but as requirements grew it was augmented by this thirty-footer, largest Pelton wheel in the world. Crankshafts drove dual compressors which delivered air at ninety pounds pressure to the Central Shaft half a mile away, where it ran hoists, pumps, drills, and the blacksmith forge. Electricity to

Splendor in the pines: Bourn owned three mansions, one in San Francisco, one on the Peninsula, and this one, designed by Willis Polk and built in the mid-nineties. At right, as seen from the road. Below, the front, viewed across a lotus pond. (3)

Farther down the road is the mine manager's residence with spacious porches well suited to hot summers. Here it is overlaid with the cool shadows of early morning. (4)

# Pennsylvania

Adjoining the Empire is the Pennsylvania, also once a great producer and in its later years part of the Empire complex. The 4600-foot inclined shaft was equipped with this hoist machinery. Dials calibrated in hundreds of feet showed the levels at which the skip stopped. Thus 46 stands for the 4600-foot level (about 1900 vertical feet down) which was the bottom of the shaft. There it was met by a crosscut tunnel from the Empire. Other corridors connected with the WYOD (Work Your Own Diggings) Mine and some extended as far as Main Street.

It was not unusual for a Grass Valley miner visiting San Francisco to ask the elevator operator to let him off at the 600 level, instead of sixth floor. (5)

16

# California Mine Bell Signals

## BASIC BELL SIGNALS

1 bell, to hoist.

1 bell, to stop if in motion.

1 bell, to release skip.

2 bells, to lower.

3 bells, man on: run slow.

7 bells, accident.

3-2-1 bells, ready to shoot in the shaft.

Each mine could and usually did add its own special signals to this list. Sign is in collection of Nevada County Historical Society.

# North

Just below the old settlement of Boston Ravine, on the banks of Wolf Creek, stands this monster Pelton wheel in the ruins of an air compressor plant built in 1895. The North Star Mine was preparing to sink the Central Shaft, and power was needed to run its machinery. Since electrical systems of the period were not considered reliable, air was chosen, and water power was to compress the air.

First an 18½-foot diameter wheel was used, but as air requirements grew it was augmented by this thirty-footer, largest Pelton wheel in the world. Crankshafts drove dual compressors which delivered air at ninety pounds pressure to the Central Shaft half a mile away, where it ran hoists, pumps, drills and the blacksmith forge. Electricity took over, and this plant ceased operations in 1933. All equipment except the big wheel (saved by private donation) was scrapped in 1959. Now the site is to be a mining museum. (6)

Above, massive hub is cast iron; the rest is steel. Original buckets were a Risdon Iron Works patent design of bronze, later replaced by more conventional ones, most of which are missing now. Buckets were divided for smoother water flow. Water at 335 pounds per square inch static pressure hissed through three 1¾-inch nozzles to turn wheel at 65 rpm. Under these conditions it developed 1000 horsepower. The flywheel effect was enormous.

# Star &

## BOSTON RAVINE

Arched stone aqueduct across Wolf Creek, which here traverses Boston Ravine, is seen through crumbling window of compressor building.

During construction of aqueduct, heavy pipe was laid down and covered with masonry. Pipeline carried water from reservoir many miles away to gain necessary pressure. (California Historical Society.)

Below, 18½-foot wheel and compressors. Belt-driven governor in right foreground regulated nozzles at bottom of pit. (Society of California Pioneers.)

The North Star vein was discovered in 1851 on the edge of Lafayette Hill (1½ miles southwest of the air compressor plant) and there an inclined shaft was sunk. In 1897 the owners sank the Central vertical shaft, which intercepted the inclined shaft twice: once 1600 feet below the surface, and again at 3500 feet, because the inclined shaft angled back as it went deeper. The celebrated Nordberg air hoist handled ore from this shaft. Deepest of all Grass Valley mines, the North Star reached a vertical depth of over 4000 feet at the 9800-foot level. Through 1928 the mine had produced $29,000,000, and one small pocket of ore, so concentrated it was brought up in candle boxes, paid $40,000.

Opposite page: Half a mile down Allison Ranch Road from Boston Ravine are foundations of 60-stamp mill that processed ore from North Star's Central Shaft. Rising in jumbled tiers of stone and concrete, these fantastic shapes suggest the combined ruins of a Mayan temple and a fortress on the Spanish Main. (7)

Beside Old Auburn Road, some distance removed from other North Star artifacts, remnants of the original shaft speak of times past. At left, headframe still juts above the waste dump; its top can be seen from the road. Foundations of hoist house are in foreground.

Below, road runs between old stonework that once supported a 40-stamp mill, used until the larger, more conveniently located Central Shaft mill was built. (8)

# On the Rhode Island Trail

The town was assuming an air of permanence and far away the Rebellion had begun when John and Bridget Polkinghorn built this home in 1861 beside the trail leading up Rhode Island Ravine, worked years earlier by the Rhode Island Company. Two years later they sold it and joined the silver rush across the Sierra to the Comstock. (9)

# On Gold Hill

Whether accomplished by an observant George McKnight chasing a stray cow or, more likely, by an unknown German stubbing his toe on a glinting outcropping, the discovery of gold-bearing quartz here in 1850 drastically changed the picture of mining in California. Probably similar finds were made elsewhere but this one created the excitement that made quartz mining a great industry. This monument, since moved to another location nearby, is shown standing on the foundations of the Gold Hill Mine, which turned out $4,000,000 in 1850-51. (10)

# From Far Lands

Here in the Catholic cemetery the monuments stand half-submerged in a sea of myrtle vines shaded by huge cedar trees. The many Irish names, the counties of the Emerald Isle from whence they came, the dates and ages at death, all reflect something of the trials of the immigrant pioneers.

Fences, first of simple design used merely to protect graves from roving cattle, later became ornate decorations in their own right. The gate above is part of an iron enclosure manufactured in San Francisco. At the center of the sunburst are initials of the Latin words meaning Jesus, Savior of Man. (11)

# Golden Center

Across Wolf Creek remnants of the Golden Center Mine gradually crumble and rust away. Most impressive equipment is the twenty-stamp mill which pulverized ore as the first step in recovering gold. Steam, later electric power, turned the massive pulleys by belt drive. Extracting gold from rock was a problem first met by pounding the quartz with a hammer. The Mexican arrastra, which ground the ore between rough stones, found favor for a while. Then came the stamp mill. The earliest mill on Wolf Creek had stamps made of logs capped with iron. Later, iron stamps in sets of five came into service.

Begun in the early 1850's as the Dromedary, and taken over in 1913 by Charles Brockington whose wife Lucy renamed it the Golden Center, this mine probed deep beneath Grass Valley's streets, tapping the Church Hill, Garage, Sleep, and Dromedary veins. Plagued by a heavy flow of water, it closed for a time, then sunk a shaft from the Scotia claim on the west side of town. A new mill there retired this one at the old workings in 1938. (12)

Above, an ore skip, rigged to dump automatically; below, switch frog rusts away. At right, one of the four batteries of stamps in the mill shown on opposite page. Replaceable iron shoes were wedged in the hollow stamps to take wear. Maker of this particular battery was famed Miners Foundry in Nevada City.

Adams & Co. first brought us the President's message, received by the Columbus. Frank Ryan, whose gallant exploits we have often recorded, carried the message from Marysville to Benecia overland. going for miles through the tules where the water was from fetlock deep to the girths, and would have arrived several hours earlier than intelligence from any other source, had not a chance boat stopped at Benecia.

The news by the Cortez the next day, and eight days later, was first handed us by Wells, Fargo & Co. The details by this arrival will be found on our to-day's first page.

---

Attention is requested to the advertisement of Grauman & Josephson, in another column.

---

The merry ringing of sleigh bells has been heard for several days past in our city. Several temporary sleighs have been fitted up, and the young gentlemen have treated the ladies to dashing turnouts. On Tuesday the Countess of Landsfeldt paid our berg a flying visit per this conveyance and a span of horses, decorated with impromptu cow bells, She flashed like a meteor through the snow flakes and wanton snowballs, and after a thorough tour of the thoroughfares, disappeared in the direction of Grass Valley.

---

SPECIMENS.—We have it on good authority that five children have been born in this city since 1854 came in, and still more are expected to appear before January goes out.

---

The snow and excessive cold of the past few days have entirely suspended all mining operations, the ditches being frozen and buried. Last night was the coldest ever known by white men in these mountains.

Social note about Lola appeared in January 20, 1854 issue of NEVADA [City] JOURNAL. (Bancroft Library.)

# Countess of Landsfeldt

Montez home was one-story cottage when she lived here; second floor was added some years later.

Lola Montez, beautiful, intelligent and spirited, arrived in California in 1853 preceded by a delicious aroma of European scandal. Irish-born in 1818, she had danced her way to success on the Continent and had dazzled lovers, two husbands and the King of Bavaria, who had taken her as mistress and titled her Countess of Landsfeldt.

In San Francisco her spider dance was a theatrical sensation until caricatured by a rival. Ridiculed, Lola and her latest husband, journalist Patrick Purdy Hull, sailed for Sacramento. There she quarreled with the theater manager, challenged him to a duel, was laughed at, and in burning indignation swept on to Marysville where the tour fizzled out. Lola and Pat boarded a stage for Grass Valley, decided it was a painfully needed refuge. They bought this home and Lola busied herself in domesticity, even tending the garden.

The town's best families shunned them, so their elegant hospitality and brilliant *salons* were lavished on a few daring citizens and a parade of out-of-town

As a hostess welcoming her guests at this door, Lola would be stunningly attired in a Paris gown and adorned with diamonds and emeralds, each reflecting the myriad lighted candles within the house. Veranda is framed by great trunks of ivy.

leading lights who found their way to the house on Mill Street. Lola may or may not have horse-whipped a local editor for disparaging her in print, as one story goes. She did, however, show yet another facet by helping the town's needy, carrying food and medicine to injured miners, keeping watch all night at the bed of a sick child, and endearing herself to many by her acts of charity.

Lola evicted Patrick Hull after a quarrel over the shooting of her pet bear. Afraid of boredom, she left Grass Valley in the summer of 1855 for a professional dance tour of Australia. She returned just long enough to sell her home, the only one she ever had owned, and to bid farewell to the town that had promised so much tranquillity. Beset by dwindling health and fortune, Lola died in New York in 1861. *(Opposite, top right: California Historical Society.)* (13)

27

As a hostess welcoming her guests at this door, Lola would be stunningly attired in a Paris gown and adorned with diamonds and emeralds, each reflecting the myriad lighted candles within the house. Veranda is framed by great trunks of ivy.

Below, Lola's pet bear and her flock of doves were sheltered here.

# Early Stonework

Almost directly across Mill Street from the Montez home is another of Grass Valley's older buildings. This stone cottage, of European flavor but Americanized by a porch, was built prior to 1855 by Thomas Hodge and has remained in the family ever since. (14)

## Faith and a Massacre

On South Church Street behind the Montez home stands Emmanuel Episcopal Church, one of the oldest religious edifices in the Northern Mines. The Gold Hill Mining Company donated the lot in 1856 with the condition that a church be erected within 18 months.

The Rev. Smeatham, third rector, was massacred by Indians in Nevada while on a church mission. As the attackers closed in, his last words were "Be as cool as though entering church." (15)

# Girl with the Red-Gold Hair

Lotta Crabtree, vivacious child with red-gold hair, merry dark eyes and carefree laugh, peered through the gate at the new occupant a few doors down Mill Street from her mother's boarding house. The Crabtrees had come to the gold fields from New York, where Lotta had been born in 1847. Now, in late summer of 1853 Lola Montez had moved into the neighborhood. Soon the attractive child was noticed by the lonely entertainer, who began teaching her intricate dance steps and found that Lotta possessed a better sense of rhythm than Lola herself. The pair often rode the countryside, the six-year-old perched in front of the saddle. At Rough and Ready, according to legend, Lotta danced on the blacksmith's anvil to the miners' loud applause.

The Crabtrees moved to Rabbit Creek (now La Porte) in Plumas County, where Lotta, at maternal urging, gave a performance that brought gold showering onto the stage. Child entertainers were a great fad, and the Crabtrees toured mining camps with growing success. Lotta went on to become the toast of theater audiences for half a century. Lola Montez, instrumental in the rise of the tiny but brilliant star, once remarked that historians would record her, Countess of Landsfeldt, as notorious but would call Lotta Crabtree famous. Lotta died in Boston in 1924, wealthy and famous. *(Above: Nevada County Historical Society.)* (16)

# Downtown Mill Street

Public library is site of birthplace of famous philospher Josiah Royce, born November 20, 1855. He went on to teach at Harvard, was especially concerned with social ethics. (17)

From the beginning, this has been the principal business thoroughfare of Grass Valley. Once it was part of a trail that led from Boston Ravine up Wolf Creek to the sawmill of James Walsh and Zenas Wheeler, then on to a junction with the beaten path (now Main Street) connecting Rough and Ready with Nevada City.

Early builders appreciated the need for sidewalks sheltered from sun, rain and snow, and much of Mill Street's charm derives from the wooden awnings. Above them rise facades out of the past, some of them brick not yet modernized, some plastered but with characteristic deep-set narrow windows accompanied by pivot eyes for iron shutters long missing.

The shutters were primarily for protection against fire. Some of these buildings were constructed after the big blaze of 1855 cleaned out more perishable predecessors, while others were erected following the conflagrations of 1860, 1862 and 1873.

Power lines and automobiles aside, Mill Street retains the atmosphere of the great mining days. (18)

Turn-of-the-century Mill Street, seen from Main, was busy and bedecked with flags, perhaps for the Fourth of July. (California Historical Society.)

Mill Street today.

# Main Street

From the steamer landings at Marysville a heavily traveled wagon road led into the mountains through Timbuctoo, Smartville and Rough and Ready, then down this street and on toward Nevada City and the remote camps along forks of the upper Yuba.

On opposite page, Main Street during the first attempt at macadamizing in 1873. The populace is searching for gold contained in the rock, which is Dromedary Mine waste material with some pieces of hight-grade ore mixed in it. To that extent was Main Street paved with gold. Above, the same scene 91 years later. (Opposite, California Historical Society.) (19)

Holbrooke Hotel, popular with travelers attending the important concerns of hydraulic mining, originally was Exchange Hotel, completed in 1862. Clues to its past may be found in such details as this iron-shuttered window in a rear wall. (20)

# South
# Church
# Street

Twin houses show stylish touch from a more graceful era. (21)

This Congregational church replaced one built in 1853 and destroyed by fire. In the previous building a Women's Temperance Union, believed to have been the first group of its kind, was organized March 25, 1874. Later the same year the national WCTU sprang into existence, whereupon the Grass Valley WTU joined its ranks. In a mining camp it was a losing cause. (22)

34

## Of Wealth and Politics

In 1867 the knowledgeable brothers Coleman, Edward and John, prosperous from North Star and other mining investments, bought the unlikely Idaho Mine, found the lost lode and produced millions. Some of the profits helped build the Nevada County Narrow Gauge, of which John was first president and Edward one of its directors. Legend says they never disagreed except over politics: one was Republican, the other Democrat, and each tried to outdo the other in promoting rallies and torchlight parades for rival candidates. Each built a fine home; this is Edward's, and his initials decorate the wrought-iron gates. (23)

Wires held up bat-like wings on this model, one of several designed by Gilmore. (Nevada County Historical Society.)

# He Sought the Sky

Gilmore Field today, with a tattered modern light plane standing on the short dirt strip. View down the runway is much the same as Gilmore saw it on his pioneering flights.

Gilmore Field, a neglected landing strip atop a hill west of Grass Valley, has only its name to remind history that here was the West's first commercial airport, the stage for early aviation experiments by an extraordinary man. While others burrowed for gold, Lyman Gilmore studied the flight of birds. He borrowed his employer's horse to tow his first glider, which sailed grandly over the animal, creating panic in it and consternation in the employer, who promptly fired him.

While Gilmore was working hard to achieve powered flight in 1903, the Wright brothers announced their success. It was a great blow; he had been certain he would be first. Nevertheless he continued his efforts and proved some of his ideas in the air. Available engines were not the equal of his vision. He built a large fuselage with an unheard-of enclosed cabin from which sprouted gracefully raked wings, but the heavy craft refused to leave the ground.

After World War I he staged flying exhibitions at his field and invited famous aviators to perform. One such was the Flying Dutchman, who would zoom through thrilling maneuvers and then offer amazed and apprehensive onlookers a ride. As an added attraction the wooden hangar filled with Gilmore's curious machines was opened to the public. It was a terrible loss when a wayfarer preparing his evening meal accidentally burned down the structure.

As an election bet, Lyman and his brother vowed they never would cut their hair until William Jennings Bryan became President. As a result he wore shoulder-length locks until he died at age 74. *(Center: Nevada County Historical Society.)* (24)

## Scotia

At the end of Carpenter Street stand the abandoned surface properties of the Scotia Claim, newer part of the Golden Center Mine. Here Cooley Butler, iron tycoon trying for gold, sunk a thousand-foot vertical shaft to connect with drifts from the old Golden Center inclined shaft. This was simply a more efficient approach to the same ore.

Dominating the scene is that ubiquitous souvenir of water power days, a discarded Pelton wheel. (25)

On the warm, quiet morning of August 31, 1942 the last scheduled train prepares to leave Grass Valley for Colfax. Number Eight, leaking wisps of steam and wearing a wartime blackout hood on her converted coal oil headlamp, waits on the main line beside trusswork of the creaky turntable. The mellowness of long years is here, and the air is fragrant with pine and sun-dried grass, pungent oil smoke and weathered creosote.

While the fireman oils valve gear the young brakeman, brakeclub in hand, stands atop the first boxcar and the engineer pauses, before mounting to the cab, perhaps thinking of other days and other runs.

In a few moments the whistle will sound a short double toot, the bell will toll briefly and the little train, freighted with memories, will chuff out of the yard and roll down shining rails into history.

Rails embedded in Kidder Avenue at Bennett Street are chief evidence remaining.

# Nevada County Narrow Gauge

Steps lead from former railroad yard to Kidder's once-ornate mansion, now remodeled.

Early stage and wagon rates to the heart of the Northern Mines were so high that public-spirited and profit-minded citizens felt the time was ripe for a rail connection with the outside world. The resulting line, completed in 1876, threaded the canyons and rolling countryside between Nevada City and Grass Valley and the Central Pacific main line at Colfax. Construction superintendent John F. Kidder laid out a 25-mile route that included steep grades, two tunnels and several trestles, the highest 95 feet above the Bear River. (Later this section was relocated using a much higher steel bridge.)

After the first woodburning iron horse steamed into town, public clamor made Kidder the line's operating superintendent. The road was a never-ending topic of local conversation and bound residents together in common appreciation or frustration. Patrons affectionately nicknamed it the "Never Come, Never Go" and "Old Man Kidder's Narrow Gauge."

Its three-foot track carried more gold (some $300,000,000 worth) than any other short line in California. Increasing highway transportation, followed by World War II mining restrictions, determined its fate: after 36 years of service the tracks were torn up, closing an era. (26)

# Gold and a Tragedy

The bitter winds of winter sweep summer's leaves across a wide grave in Elm Ridge Cemetery, and the sun strikes through lowering clouds to illuminate an inscription that barely hints at tragic fate.

Michael Brennan, a man of education and refined sensibilities, was sent from New York to superintend operations of the Mount Hope Mining Company on Massachusetts Hill. At first successful, he presently encountered defeats that made him feel he had let down those who had invested money and confidence in his management. The rich strike eluded him.

On Sunday morning, February 22, 1858, the bodies of the entire family were discovered in their home. Brennan had administered Prussic acid to his wife and three small children, then to himself. He left a letter saying he could not bear to see his family living in poverty and disgrace and wishing that he might take with him on his long journey his mother and sister, who were living in Europe and were dependent on him.

Much litigation followed and the mine was closed. In 1863 it was reopened and in April 1864 the Massachusetts Hill Company, working at the bottom of Brennan's shaft only a few feet from where he had abandoned work, struck the ledge Brennan had sought. (27)

# Idaho-Maryland

Little remains of this illustrious mine except these rotting wooden tanks. After the ore was finely crushed by ball mills, the pulp was allowed to flow into this set of tanks where the precious metal was leached out by cyanidation.

The Idaho was discovered in 1863 but little work was done until 1867 when the Coleman brothers bought it, organized the Idaho Quartz Mining Company, sunk a shaft and struck a continuation of the Eureka ore shoot, an especially notable ledge. Exploiting this, the mine produced $12,000,000 and paid $6,000,000 in steady dividends up to 1893. Then dwindling ore reserves, and a dispute with the adjacent Maryland Mine over claim to the Eureka shoot, led the Colemans to retire and sell the Idaho to the Maryland. The combined mines proved a hoodoo to their next several operators, who dropped large sums of money trying to find paydirt. Finally the formation of the Idaho-Maryland Mines Company drew the smiles of Lady Luck, new ore came to light and the enterprise employed a thousand men through the lucrative 1930's. (28)

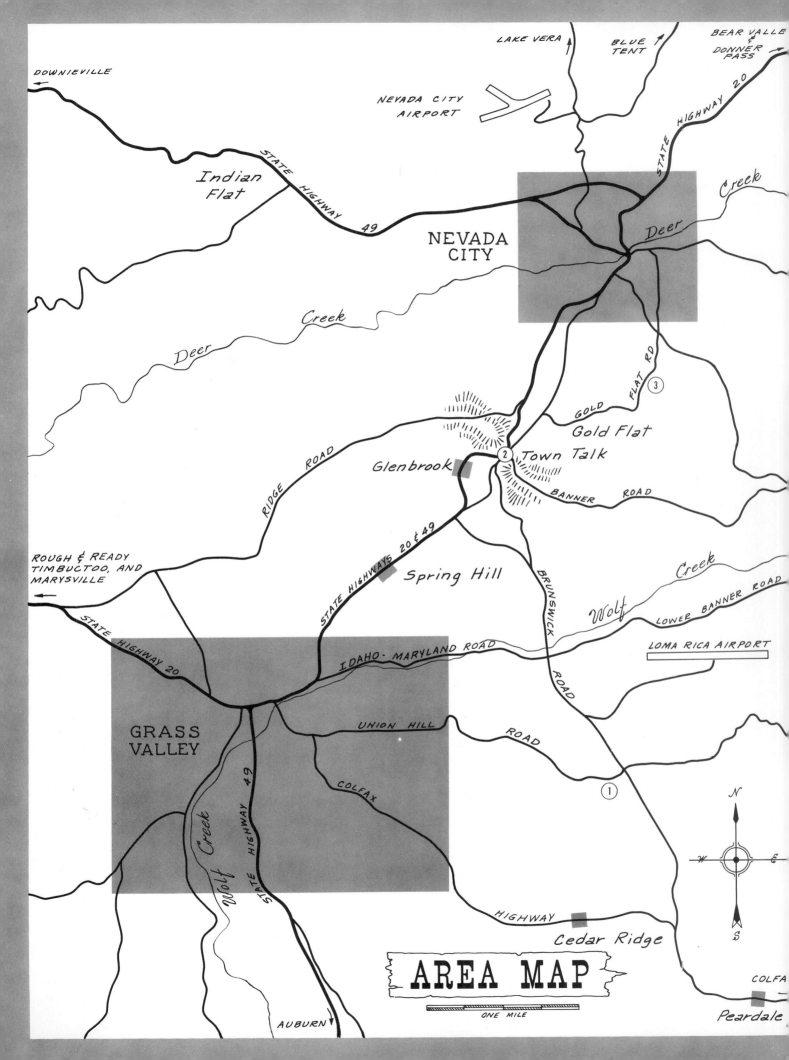

# New Brunswick

Rising in monolithic grandeur out of a lumberyard is a concrete silo more reminiscent of grain than of gold. This unique headframe contains a circular ore bin and a square housing down which the skip descended into the shaft. At left is a wall of the hoist building. On a nearby hill was the original Brunswick, one of the earliest workings in the district. In 1915 New Brunswick's vertical shaft was sunk and 900 feet down encountered the old inclined shaft. At right are some of thousands of exploratory drill cores. (Area map 1)

1857 advertisement in NEVADA [City]
JOURNAL. (Bancroft Library.)

The pass at Town Talk became inter-
section for six roads.

# The Pass to the Other Side

Those making the journey between Grass Valley and
Nevada City must surmount a steep ridge that divides
the Wolf Creek and Deer Creek watersheds. Roads as-
cend the lower slopes by separate ways and then con-
verge to pass through the notch at Town Talk. In all
likelihood this was an ancient route, for centuries
familiar to Indians following game trails.

Then, in a flash of intrusion, the forty-niners found
it; a wagon road to the far reaches of the Northern
Mines passed through it; the narrow gauge tunneled

just below its summit, and a streetcar line crawled
over the top. The freeway is cutting through here,
where a moment ago in the long scheme of things
tribesmen walked softly in the tracks of deer and
grizzlies.

From the gap a panorama spreads out to the east,
and pine-fringed hills give way to a grassy hollow.
A grove of poplars marks the site of Gold Flat, once
an Indian campground, later the location of gold refining operations. (Area map 2)

View over Gold Flat in early
winter. In foreground, snowberries
dot lush meadowgrass; in middle
distance, aromatic smoke trails
into the crisp air as residents perform seasonal ritual of burning
pine needles; and on the horizon
the Sierra crest gleams with its
first heavy mantle of snow.

44

Hidden on a side road off Gold Flat Road is a remarkable relic of the Sneath and Clay Mine. Water was an eternal problem, and a vast assortment of pumping machinery was evolved over the years. Quite popular was the Cornish system, in which a rod down the mine shaft simultaneously operated a series of pumps. Each pump delivered its load of water into a tank from which the next higher pump drew its supply. The idea is said to have originated in Cornwall in 1801.

Pumprods were iron or wood, generally wood. A section might be 16 inches square and seventy feet long. Sections could be joined to form a pumprod up to 3000 feet long. The pump engine commonly was hooked up to a walking beam (see picture) that in turn pushed the pumprod. This is the last Cornish pump known to exist hereabouts. The Sneath and Clay started in 1862, closed in 1867, reopened under the name Phoenix in 1916 and eventually gave up for good, leaving this legacy. (Area map 3)

Looking down from headframe into shaft of Sneath and Clay Mine. Pump is on right side.

# The Cornish Pump

# NEVADA CITY

Beside the turbulent waters of Deer Creek there sprang up a settlement that is still the most complete gold town left in California, a rich amalgam of brick business buildings, tidy homes and handsome mansions that from the earliest times lent it the shape and character of a metropolis.

Like Rome and San Francisco, Nevada City was built on seven hills and then a few. Its precipitous location and heady beginnings were effectively described by a pioneer editor in 1852: "The city is upon the hillsides, on the ridges, among the streams and over them; the muddy water rushing beneath houses, stores and hotels and through the streets, splashing and gurgling as if uttering self-congratulatory hymns for its escape from the torturing cradles, long toms and sluices.

"Not until a personal observation of the natural riches of Nevada [City] had I anything like an adequate conception of its golden abundance. Our people have scarcely passed the threshold of the auriferous palaces, richer in treasures than the Arabian Nights. The amount of gold taken from the placer diggings in this vicinity during two years would almost stagger belief could it be stated."

Leading the vanguard were three young miners by the names of Pennington, Cross and Mc-Caig who put up a cabin at the confluence of Gold Run and Deer Creek in the fall of 1849. Others were on their heels. Dr. A. B. Caldwell opened a store farther upstream and the handiest title for the burgeoning camp became Caldwell's Upper Store, although Deer Creek Dry Diggings was used almost simultaneously. In 1850, with the population already over 6,000, a mass meeting was held and a new name picked: Nevada. This prevailed until

47

the creation of the territory of Nevada in 1861 forced the town to distinguish itself by adding the word City. The county took its name from the town, which became the seat of government.

The fifties were the building years as 15,000 miners and supporting entourage of families and shopkeepers crowded into the area to profit from placer, hydraulic and quartz mining. Seven devastating fires swept the town and each time it was rebuilt they used more brick. From its inception Nevada City took on an organized and sophisticated tone lacking in most other mining camps. This stemmed from a concentration of New England moral influence and from the fact the town's leaders were remarkably able and responsible men who stamped an imprint of law on a social fabric little noted for its inhibitions.

Beginnings of Hearst fortune came from Lecompton Mine in the wilds of Deer Creek above Nevada City. George Hearst located mine in 1858, produced $60,000 in 20 months and left to join silver rush to the Comstock. The sacks contain high-grade ore. (Nevada County Historical Society.)

Exuberance was not missing altogether: saloons were indeed plentiful, there were a few shootings (on occasion punished by legal hangings), and it was not always wise to travel nearby roads unarmed. The cast of characters included pretty Mme. Eleanore Dumont, better known as Madame Moustache, who for two years ran a genteel gambling parlor. And it is true, for once, that Mark Twain was here, albeit only to lecture on the Sandwich Islands.

More impressive, however, was the number of strong-willed pioneers who built a community after the Eastern manner and who founded fortunes and families destined to be interwoven with the development of the West; their names and accomplishments would be a book in itself.

The town's random street pattern is inherited from the days when the plaza was the business center from which pack trails led out to the various

49

diggings by the most expedient routes. In time these became wagon roads and finally were paved.

Seasons are sharply distinct. Winter brings frost, bright days, cold rains, rarely snow; spring urges old orchards into bloom, wild sweetpea climbs flaking stonework, and great lilac bushes brought from the East in covered wagons fill door-yards with their fragrance. As summer comes in, Scotch broom splashes yellow on the hillsides and deciduous trees swallow houses in a burst of greenery. Then autumn, when Nevada City is in its glory: maples, planted by early settlers in memory of eastern childhoods, blaze forth in reds and oranges; Lombardy poplars become slim golden torches.

And if you listen closely in the mountain dusk, as wood smoke curls from chimneys and stove-pipes, you may hear a distant jangle of harness, spatter of hoofs and rumble of wheels as the stage from Red Dog, You Bet and Liberty Hill rolls down to the Deer Creek crossing in some long-ago twilight.

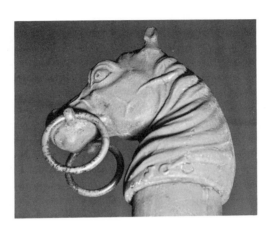

Soon to be cut down for a freeway is this living monument to a pioneer's planting. For years it has been decorated with lights each Christmas-tide, welcoming home the weary traveler. (1)

# Here the Wagons, There the Beer

Sacramento Street curves gently down to the town plaza and the two bridges over Deer Creek. Traffic did not enter by this route in Nevada City's first years but used a log bridge farther downstream. Several trails converged at what is now the plaza, however, and a footbridge let business expand onto the small flat this side of the creek. In 1853 this road was gouged out of the steep bank to connect with two new wagon spans across Deer Creek. Travel then came this way.

The old stone brewery (at right; now a cafe) was one of several local brewhouses that formerly slaked the population's thirst in a land of hot, dry summers.

At the corner of Sacramento and Boulder Streets, at the edge of the plaza where there is now a gas station, once stood the Adams Express Company office and next to it the Phoenix Saloon. Established in 1851, Adams did well for a while, shipped gold to the Atlantic states and Europe, then collapsed in 1854, leaving the field to Wells, Fargo & Co. (2)

# National Hotel

Dominating lower Broad Street, the National Exchange, as it first was called, became the hub of commerce for the Northern Mines. In its former lobby (now dining room) were the clicking sounders of the telegraph office and the bustling headquarters of stage lines and Wells Fargo Express.

Hard-grubbed fortunes were gambled away easily in the old barroom, which boasted a Honduras mahogany bar still used in the present establishment.

Between the hotel and its annex runs National Alley, scene of a curious duel in 1853. Billy Mason had been defeated for the state assembly seat, largely by the efforts of H. C. Gardiner. Enraged, Mason challenged Gardiner, weapons to be revolvers. Without benefit of seconds the skirmish began, Gardiner standing squarely in the middle of Broad Street, Mason hiding in the alley shadows and popping out to shoot. By the time the guns were empty each man was shot in the leg, the serenity of a nearby printing office had been shattered by a stray bullet, and a pig that had the temerity to cross between the duelists had become an innocent victim.

The main part of the National consists of four conjoined buildings (look at the facades) put up in 1856-7. Previously the site was occupied by a log jail, from which Rattlesnake Dick escaped only to be killed later by a posse. And for decades, shadowy National Alley led to large stables of stage horses and other more gaudy stables of *filles de joie*. (3)

At left above, lobby clock has served generations of travelers. At left, a busy cluster of stages in bygone days. (Left: Nevada County Historical Society.)

Opposite page, a glass-walled bridge leads from main hotel over National Alley to the annex with its turnip dome. Duel was fought here.

52

# Broad Street — Then and Now

In the above 1857 view down Broad Street, Pine Street intersects from the left between the white wooden balcony and the brick building just beyond. The photographer's long focal length lens compressed distances, making Pine seem narrower than it actually was. Signs include Justice's Court next to City Brewery, What Cheer House Restaurant below American Livery Stable, and farther down a panel depicting a flamboyant lady on horseback.

The same scene today, below, reveals balconies gone but iron shutters still in place. Signs are neon, there are tourists on the corner instead of miners; yet it has not changed too much in 107 years. (*Above, Nevada City Public Library.*) (4)

54

This was Nevada City's second thoroughfare and lots were staked out by May, 1850. Chinese began to arrive by 1851 and first settled above town in Manzanita Ravine. Gradually they established businesses along upper Commercial Street to form this Chinatown. The small shops were filled with the goods and life patterns of the distant Orient, set down in a great gold camp amidst alien mountains. Opium dulled hardships and loneliness.

One of the last enterprises to remain was a laundry (left) with its attic door opening onto a missing balcony. More recent occupants of time-worn structures are shoveling out after a rare heavy snow. (5)

# Down Commercial Street: Chinatown

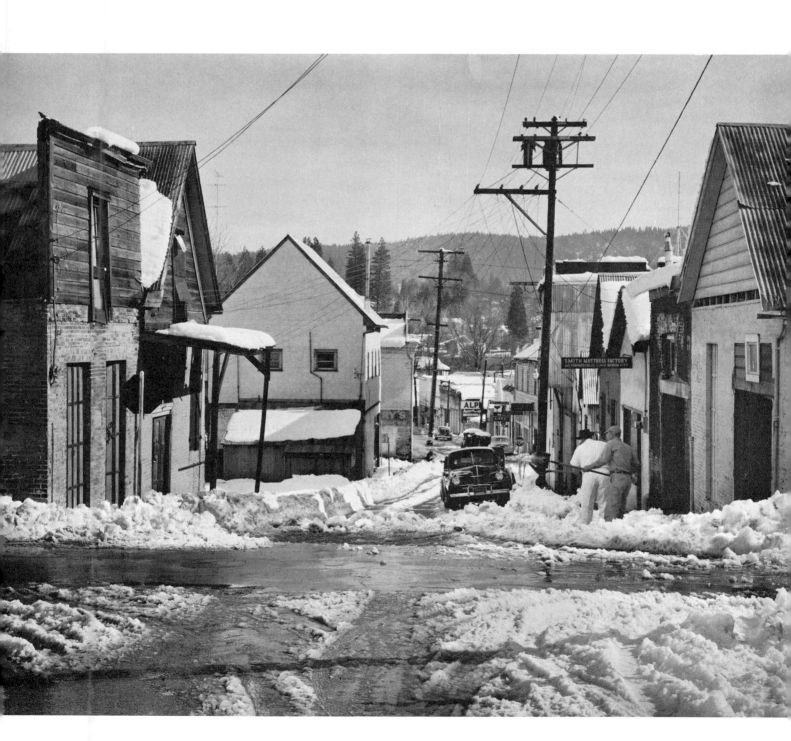

## The Retreat

At the corner of Commercial and Pine, Williamson and Blaze opened a saloon that became a favorite of professional men in old Nevada City. It was said that if one wanted to listen in on intellectual conversation, one should go to Blaze's.

The original establishment was on the opposite corner from the present sign; there was no neon in those days, and Pine Street (pictured) was planked, not paved. But there were rainy nights like this, the elements shutting down the world without, when a prudent man might choose a warm stove, refreshments, and illuminating conversation. (6)

# Memories and Iron Shutters

The lower end of Commercial Street, slanting into Main Street, was the center of town in the early years. The present post office stands on the site of an old store that replaced the Womack and Kenzie Hotel, a cloth affair that vanished in the fire of 1851. Commercial Street followed the banks of Oregon Ravine, and whenever a lot was excavated for a foundation, a miner could be found at the stream hopefully washing the dirt for gold. Brick buildings began to go up in 1853, and here they wall in the street much as in former times. Iron shutters on the second stories tell the tale.

The brick was local, coming from the Nevada Brick Yard which began operations at the head of Broad Street in 1851. (Brick vaults were installed in many banks and hotels to safeguard valuables.) Ironwork, especially items not directly useful in the mines, had to be imported for the first several years and even later. The Union Iron Works and Pacific Iron Works of San Francisco supplied gold rush towns with iron doors and shutters, whose main purpose usually was not to bar scoundrels but to seal apertures when a nearby fire threatened. A layer of earth or broken brick on the roof completed protective measures. (7)

Nevada Hose Company began building its red brick home in April, 1861. As finished, it sported a white Greek facade which later was removed when the Victorian bell tower and gingerbread trim were added. Hose carts first were pulled by men, later by horses. Competing express companies in town had a standing order to rush their horses to firehouses when an alarm sounded; the first to hitch a horse to a hose cart and speed it to the fire received $2.50. At night, a nearby livery stable kept in readiness a horse with singletree harness in place. Eventually the hose companies acquired their own horses, and a stable was added to the rear of Firehouse No. 1, with connecting door to the equipment.

A big gelding called Nick was one of a long line of fire horses to pull the ladder wagon. When he found inactivity between fires boring, he would force the stable lock with his teeth, go to the front of the firehouse and pull on the dangling fire bell rope. By the time the excited volunteers arrived, Nick would be standing between the shafts of the ladder wagon eagerly waiting to be hitched. Even after he was sold to a laundry for delivery use, the fire bell would bring him galloping to the scene, laundry wagon, sputtering driver and all.

Now the firehouse is the museum of the Nevada County Historical Society. (8)

# Firehouse
# No. 1

Joss house altar is displayed inside, along with many other relics of pioneering times. The museum is open every day from May 31 through Labor Day, and only on special occasions the rest of the year.

# A Comstock Reminder

Imagine the enthusiasm of a group of young men establishing a new town! It was exciting to be one of the founders and a part of its growth, and so they looked for a place to begin. The only level spot of any size for a main street lay between Deer Creek and today's post office. Here these young men put up crude shelters of logs, shakes and canvas and confidently bestowed on them such designations as Empire Hotel, Barker's Exchange and Tattersall Stables. Main Street continued up the hill on the trail that led to the mines of Selby Flat and the ridge country.

After numerous fires many of the wooden buildings were replaced with ones of brick. So constructed in 1854 was the drug store later occupied by Ott's Assay Office. It was James J. Ott, a Swiss immigrant, who in 1859 proved that ore from across the Sierra had a fabulous silver content, thus triggering the stampede to the Comstock Lode. Two Grass Valley metallurgists independently confirmed the historic assay.

Next door, edged with filigree balcony railing, stands the office of the South Yuba Canal Company, which furnished all-important water to the gravel mines of Nevada City and such diggings as Blue Tent, Quaker Hill and You Bet. The Coyote and Deer Creek Water Company, formed in 1850, was the nucleus for this wide-spread and profitable system. (9)

Many of the early-day business houses were named sentimentally after the proprietor's place of origin. Thus the Galena & Dubuque House, Buckeye Lunch & Bakery, Iowa Store, Virginia House, and the surviving New York Hotel, last of the long litany of titles that once reminded all and sundry of their eastern ties.

This notable establishment first offered rest and solace in the dusty summer of 1853, and was rebuilt after the fires of 1856 and 1863. In its final years, in the 1950's, it masqueraded under the name of Deer Creek Inn. *(At left, Bancroft Library.)* (10)

Optimists and purveyors of culture quickly set up shop in Nevada City. The above specimens, long gone, were on the corner site now occupied by a Purity store directly across Broad Street from the New York Hotel. At the left of Mme. Falcot & Co.'s inn stands the National Gymnasium, with a small sign advising that it quarters—of all things—a fencing club. While the hotel title appears a shade pretentious, the proprietess probably followed local custom in using her hometown name.

The appearance of *A4* instead of *As* in the advertisement seems merely to have been a typographical error of generous proportions. *(Above, Nevada City Public Library; right, Bancroft Library.)*

61

# Machinery
# to Mine the Gold

Just as the gold mines of Nevada County made the area world-famous for its wealth, so did the Miners Foundry become acclaimed for its ability to produce the machinery necessary to extract the precious metal. Under its grimy roof was perfected an invention that revolutionized the generation of power throughout the world.

The shop began as the Nevada Foundry at the rear of the National Hotel in 1855. After the fire of 1856 the plant was moved to its present site. When hydraulic mining was at its height, the Foundry did $30,000 worth of work in one month alone for one customer, the North Bloomfield Company. Mechanics hammered out machinery to manufacture the pipe, valves and nozzles required for huge volumes of water at high pressure. During the quartz mining days, milling equipment became a specialty. Nearly all the principal mills in the surrounding mines had their essentials built here. Notable were the patent mill guide installed in the Tonopah Mining Company's 100-stamp mill at Millers, Nevada, and a gadget known as the Miners Foundry Ejector which was in universal demand. Casting of metal meant a large area devoted to the art of pattern-making. Patterns are kept in a separate room to guard against loss, and in the formerly extensive collection were several sizes of the Pelton water wheel.

Lester Allan Pelton was one of many skilled craftsmen trying to improve on the old hurdy-gurdy wheel. In 1878, in nearby Camptonville, he invented a bucket shaped so that water would flow away smoothly after expending most of its energy pushing the wheel. Further development in Miners Foundry produced a model that was successfully tested on Deer Creek. Much of the electricity used today comes from generators driven by direct descendants of that original Pelton wheel. (11)

Pelton wheel rests beside smelting furnace.

Giant wooden crane pivots in front of century-old stonework of machine shop entrance. Cavernous gloom is penetrated by tiny splashes of sunlight.

# Firehouse
# No. 2

Eureka Hose Company No. 2 was organized in June 1860 and purchased its first fire engine from Pennsylvania Company No. 12 in San Francisco. The engine was shipped on a river boat to Marysville, thence by freight wagon to Nevada City, where the Eureka Hose boys were dismayed to find the name 'Pennsylvania' still inscribed on the machine. They quickly solved this dilemma by changing their company name to Pennsylvania. With the completion of this firehouse in the fall of 1861, they were in business.

Volunteers were proud, eager to be first at a blaze, fond of splendid uniforms and always ready to challenge other companies to contests of strength and skill. In the pose pictured above the men are holding rope, not hose. The anchor man at right wears a special harness, the captain moodily clasps his voice trumpet, and all display polished belt buckles emblazoned with the figure 2. (*Above: Nevada County Historical Society.*) (12)

# The Fighting Parson

Methodist services first were held under the open sky in the summer of 1850. Next year a church was built far up the hill on West Broad Street, with a cemetery in back. The minister, Reverend Bland, was anything but that. Dismayed to find that some husbands escorted their wives to the church door, then repaired to gambling dens downtown, he bitterly chastised these miscreants in a sermon. He also advised moving the church closer in, the better to battle Satan.

During the move to the present site a gentleman named Miller, one of those listed on the sermon roll-call, savagely attacked the minister. With giant hands the muscular Rev. Bland seized his opponent and threw him to the ground. Thoroughly humiliated, Miller had the minister arrested for assault. Miners and town riffraff jammed the courtroom, rooting for the fighting parson. Old Zeke, stern-visaged Justice of the Peace, reached a speedy decision: "I think it was a fair fight. Miller commenced it and got a good licking. The prisoner is discharged!" Whereupon there was a loud burst of applause and the Justice was treated to drinks.

After fires destroyed Bland's church and its successors, the present edifice was erected in 1864. (13)

# Nabob

Even in mining towns tucked away in the mountains it was not long until groupings of affluence and station became evident, and this was especially true of Nevada City, a metropolis in miniature. The upper reaches of Broad Street were favored by many prominent citizens, who enjoyed such residences as these. (14)

## THE HEALER

This home was remodeled and the rear garden landscaped to its present appearance by I. U. Bennetts, remembered as one of Nevada City's colorful pioneer physicians. Note the coast redwood (Sequoia sempervirens) at right of house, out of its foggy element but thriving.

## THE MINING MAN AND THE LAW-MAKER

Built after the 1863 fire, this dwelling once was occupied by Capt. Thomas Mein, noted mining man, whose son William Wallace became similarly famous. Later it was owned for decades (until 1959) by the family of the late U. S. Representative Harry Englebright.

## THE ASSAYER

Best-known owner of this house was Emil Ott, who returned to Nevada City in 1907 to carry on the assay business of his esteemed father.

# Hill

### THE MYSTERY

Stained glass embellishes this solid residence wedged in the split of East and West Broad Streets. Its builder in the early eighties was Charles E. Mulloy, mining man, half-owner of the Nevada GAZETTE and one of the town's leading grocers. The house was a source of great pride to him. He was active in civic, fraternal and political affairs and the very picture of the respected, well-liked community leader and family man.

Nevada City thus was profoundly shocked when one day Charles Mulloy hanged himself, leaving an aura of mystery surrounding the imposing home on the hill.

67

# When Emma Nevada Came Home

The great coloratura soprano Emma Nevada was born Emma Wixom, daughter of a doctor at the Alpha Hydraulic Mine above Nevada City, in 1859. Mother and child wintered in town during the sixties, once staying at the house on East Broad Street shown here. Emma gave her first public performance at the age of three, when she stood on a chair in church with the American flag draped around her and sang *The Star Spangled Banner*.

Much of her girlhood was spent in the state of Nevada, and probably she chose her stage name both for the town and the state she loved. After graduating from Mills Seminary in Oakland she studied voice in Vienna and made her stage debut in 1880. Triumphal tours of Europe and marriage in Paris followed.

The Continent conquered, Emma returned to steal the heart of Nevada City. As the Narrow Gauge steamed into the depot thousands of miners and townspeople cheered, and the band struck up *Home Sweet Home*. At the National Hotel the throng had increased in numbers. Her room (number 11) was filled with flowers. From the hotel balcony Emma waved to her admirers and applauded the band when it rendered *Auld Lang Syne*.

Next evening the Nevada Theater was packed to the doors. The tiny diva, dazzling in a cloud of sky-blue lace set off by a corsage of pink roses, and carrying a full-bloomed pink rose in her hands, stepped between the drapes to a roar of applause. Her sweet, precise voice enchanted the house, and when she closed her program with *The Last Rose of Summer*, a favorite of the times, the audience went wild.

Thus did Nevada City welcome its illustrious daughter, and thus did she gratefully respond.

Emma died in London on June 20, 1940, while German bombs burst overhead. (*At left below, Nevada County Historical Society.*) (15)

Austin home today. The front porch quite likely was added not long after 1857 photograph (at left below) was taken.

At right below, April cherry blossoms are bright against weathered barn in Roger Williams Ravine.

## On Lost Hill

Bennett Street dips across Roger Williams Ravine (presumably christened by prospecting Rhode Islanders) to the lower end of Lost Hill, already mined out by 1852. Among the residences that soon replaced the shanties was the Nora Austin home, one of the oldest in Nevada City, its honest lines still challenging sun and storm. In the ravine, cherry and plum blossoms add radiance in their season, and Lombardy poplars turn to newly-minted gold in frosty October. *(Below: Nevada City Public Library.)* (16)

# Pioneer Cemetery

In the New England tradition of placing a burial ground behind a house of worship, this cemetery was established on a knoll rising back of the original Methodist church in 1851. Many early citizens, usually sent to join the silent majority by violence, plagues or accidents, were laid to rest here under the pines, giving the site its name. Here, briefly, are stories of three of those pioneers. (17)

## Sutter's Son

All of General Sutter's family had left Switzerland and joined him in California by early 1850. William Alphonse, the youngest son, was then 17 years old. His father's holdings around Sutter's Fort had been seized by greedy forty-niners, and the family settled at Hock Farm, a surviving property north of Sacramento.

Alphonse sought livelier pursuits. After Governor Bigler appointed him aide with rank of colonel, young Sutter raised a company and took it to Nicaragua to assist the notorious adventurer Walker in revolutionary schemes. These failed, and Alphonse returned to California to dabble in Anaheim vineyards. In April 1863, ill with consumption or some tropical disease, he journeyed home to Hock Farm.

Hoping that mountain air would restore his health, he came to live with his uncle James J. Ott in Nevada City. (Ott, the reknowned assayer, was a first cousin of General Sutter.) It was not enough, and here Alphonse died, leaving a wife and young child. At the funeral in the Congregational church on Main Street in the late afternoon of August 16, 1863, a crowd of townspeople paid tribute to this favorite son of John Augustus Sutter, whose fort once had been a beacon for a westering nation. (*Above right: Sutter's Fort State Historical Monument.*)

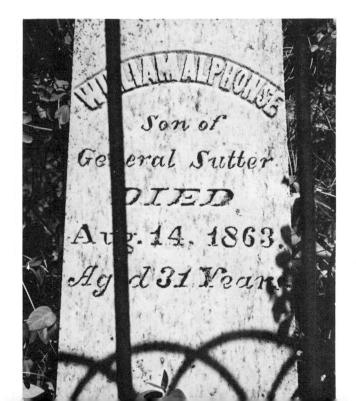

71

# An Echo of Lincoln

After a voyage around the Horn, ambitious Aaron A. Sargent rode into Nevada City in 1851, edited newspapers, brought his Massachusetts bride west, and became a force of law and order in the town's chaotic early years. In rapid succession he became lawyer, county district attorney, delegate to the national convention that nominated Lincoln, U. S. Congressman, Senator, and finally Minister to Germany.

Returning, he tried for another Senate term but was outmaneuvered by Leland Stanford. Dispirited, he practiced law in San Francisco, where he died and was entombed in 1887. When that city's Laurel Hill cemetery was used for building purposes, Sargent's ashes were scattered over his Quaker Hill mining claims and his vault was moved here as a monument to his pioneering deeds. *(Right: Bancroft Library.)*

AARON AUGUSTUS SARGENT
BORN AT
NEWBURYPORT MASS SEPTEMBER 28TH 1827
DIED AT
SAN FRANCISCO CAL AUGUST 14TH 1887

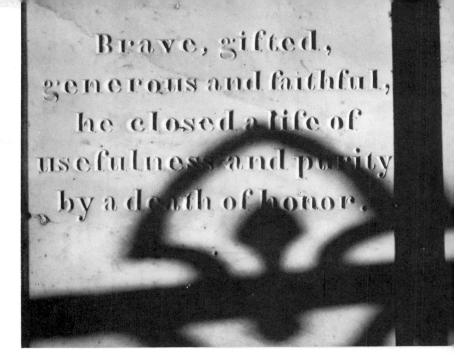

Brave, gifted, generous and faithful, he closed a life of usefulness and purity by a death of honor.

# Home From the Indian Wars

The handsome young Virginian Henry Meredith arrived in the early fifties to practice law, and soon became one of Nevada City's favorite sons. Then the cry of silver in the Comstock drew him into the rush across the Sierra in 1860, as snow melted in the passes.

A few weeks later alarm swept the Comstock: Piute Indians had massacred seven white men not far away, and Virginia City itself was rumored in danger. Uproar, a call to arms; and Meredith joined Major Ormsby's punitive expedition. Old friend Bill Stewart (see page 93) implored him not to go, but Meredith felt it his duty.

Two companies totaling a hundred men rode toward Pyramid Lake after the marauders, who neatly ambushed their pursuers in a pass. Meredith was shot and fell from his horse. His comrades offered to recover his mount so he could escape but he refused to let them imperil their lives. Finally some thirty Indians rushed Meredith with knives.

When news of his fate reached Nevada City, Captain Van Hagen mustered his little militia of twenty men, the Nevada Rifles, and led them across the mountains. During renewed battles the Rifles recovered Meredith's body. Upon their return, citizens met them outside town and formed a solemn procession to escort Henry Meredith home. *(At left above: Nevada County Historical Society.)*

# Coyote Diggings

Early prospectors started at the lower ends of the ravines draining into Deer Creek and gradually worked up them. Miners nearing the top of Manzanita Ravine in 1850 were surprised to find the gold-laden gravels extending into the sides of the hill. Unknowingly they had tapped an ancient buried river bed, evidence of a gigantic flow eons before the present stream system came into existence. In the channel were quantities of gold.

The news spread like wildfire and the rush was on. Tents, rough cabins and nondescript shelters went up at the new diggings, and the miners agreed on 30x30 foot claims. Although old hands at placer (stream) mining, here they were green and had to improvise. Shallow shafts were dug through the overlying earth to the river bed beneath, and the paydirt raised to the surface by windlass and bucket. One claim produced $40,000 in less than a month.

Soon the landscape was dotted with holes resembling coyote burrows, hence the name. The pits later were washed away by hydraulic mining, whose scars mark the site along the cut-off road joining Highways 20 and 49, on the northern outskirts of Nevada City. You can drive on the path used by the miners by following Coyote Street, once the main trail from town to Coyoteville. (18)

Opposite: This rare Daguerreotype taken at Coyoteville in October, 1850 is a classic portrait of youthful adventurers seeking their fortunes in the gold fields. On the left J. Sewall Reed reads a letter, a treasured commodity in those times. Washing paydirt in a tub to conserve water is E. D. Wadsworth. Their companions, names unknown, man the windlass over a shaft that goes down about 30 feet to drifts running out into the rich earth.

Reed later commanded the California Hundred which formed part of the 2nd Massachusetts Cavalry during the Civil War. He was killed in far-off Virginia by Mosby's Guerrilas. Wadsworth returned east eventually became treasurer of the Boston Marine Society; thus did many have their fling and go back to their homelands. (California Historical Society.)

Coyote diggings today. The crinkled surface is covered largely by manzanita and by Scotch broom, which puts on a brilliant show of yellow blossoms in early June.

Every conceivable kind of crude mining implement appears in this contemporary sketch of the hustle and bustle at Coyoteville. (California Division of Mines and Geology.)

Coyote diggings

Dwarfed by a cliff of their own making, monitors in this typical hydraulic mine are showing off for the camera. Normally water was played against the base of the bluff to cave down gold-bearing gravel. The large gas lamp, permitting night operations, replaced the primitive iron pitch-basket (opposite page) which used pine knots for fuel and scarcely touched Sierra darkness in the vast pits. (Above: Morgan North Collection; Drawing: Neils C. Tonnesen.)

# They Washed Away Mountains

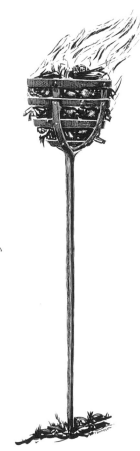

Miners, being an ingenious lot, found they could get at buried river gravels on a grand scale by piping water at high pressure through a nozzle called a giant, or monitor. From a rawhide hose used in the early 1850's by Anthony Chabot (of Oakland fame), the monitor evolved into a cannon-like monster weighing up to a ton, swiveling to reach its prey and having a business end as much as ten inches in diameter. This device could wash away entire hillsides, the mud being run through sluiceboxes to recover gold. Riverbeds all the way into the Sacramento Valley became choked with debris thus artificially eroded from the mountains. Flooded lowlanders rose in fury, resulting in the Sawyer court decision of 1884 that supposedly halted all operations except those able to contain their debris. Pockets of illegal hydraulicking went merrily on even as valley spies prowled the hostile hills, until in time the law prevailed.

Most spectacular of all hydraulic mines was the huge Malakoff (now a State park) at North Bloomfield on the San Juan Ridge.

Small giant throws an arc into Deer Creek during demonstration at Nevada City plaza. Box at back end is loaded with rocks as counterweight.

The mementos of the past shown on this and the opposite page, together with sweeping views of the lower Sierra, can be found on a side trip to the top of the ridge rising north of Nevada City.

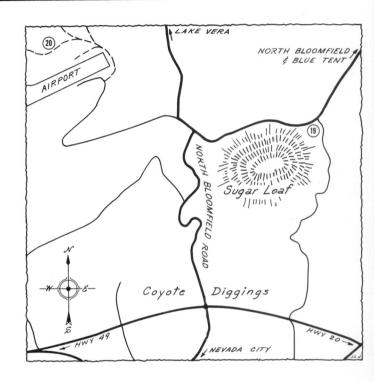

# To Feed the Monitors

Hydraulic mining required vast amounts of water, and hundreds of miles of ditches and flumes diverted the flow of creeks and rivers into reservoirs and the giant nozzles. Large dams were built far back in the mountains to store melting snow. Yet the mines consumed so much water that full operations were limited to the wet season. One example will indicate the prodigious thirst: a five-inch nozzle under a 400-foot head spewed out 11,250 gallons every minute.

This flume is one of the oldest remaining, and carries water for domestic purposes. Here it crosses the gap on the eastern shoulder of Sugar Loaf. Nearby is a monument noting the passage through this same gap of emigrant wagon trains that had come over Donner Pass and down the Harmony Ridge route.

(19)

# The Brave
# Sheriff

On the lonely ridge behind the airport, a dirt road winds to the monument marking the site of a tragic gun fight. The plaque is titled *Sheriff David Fulton Douglass*, and tells this story: "On this spot Sheriff Douglass, a native son of the golden West, gave his life July 26, 1896. Bravely performing his duty, alone he tracked a highwayman to this retreat and both fell in battle. It is believed Douglass was pitted against two and then one escaped. The bodies lay parallel."

Douglass, California-born in 1858, had been elected and reelected to his position by handsome majorities. Prior to that he guarded gold shipments on the Nevada County Narrow Gauge and the Southern Pacific's Donner Pass route as a Wells Fargo messenger. Still earlier he rode shotgun for Wells Fargo. (20)

# Medicine Rock

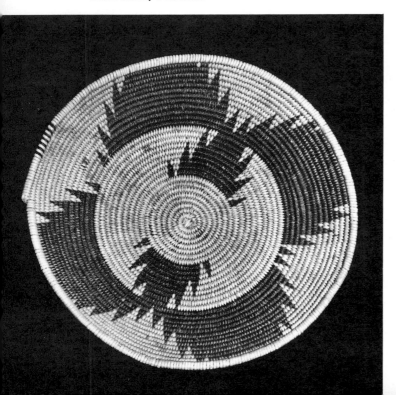

Maidu basket in Nevada County Historical Society's museum.

Indians of Nevada County were part of the Maidu Nation, which roamed from the Sacramento Valley to the crest of the Sierra Nevada. Acorns were a staple food. At the start of the gold rush there were 14 Indian campoodies (camps) within a two-mile radius of Nevada City.

One of the largest, a camp at Indian Flat, was led by old Chief Oustamah, whose name meant Swift Runner. He became a great friend of the young pioneers, and the local I.O.O.F. lodge was named for him. Indians from his camp became known as the Oustamahs, and eventually all Indians in the Nevada City area were called that.

The huge granite boulder on East Broad Street was favored by Indians in pain. The hollow on top was a perfect place to lie and soak up the sun's heat. The aborigines came to prefer the white man's hot water bottle, however, and the medicine rock finally was abandoned. (21)

# Down Main Street: Childhood Memories

Fond recollections abide in this deep-set home and high boardwalk fronting the spacious grounds. The house was built by druggist Edward Spence in 1866 on a three-lot site. Later it was acquired by Judge and Mrs. Searls as a wedding gift for their son Fred and his bride, whose six children had such a grand time growing up in old Nevada City that, although scattered now, they still maintain the home and boardwalk. (Roots are deep: Fred Searls, Jr. is chairman of the Newmont Mining Corporation, owner of the Empire-Star.) In autumn the walk is dappled with leaves, squirrels are busy, and the maples planted by Judge Searls and his son blaze with glory. (22)

# Law and a Strong Jail

This clean-lined old home at the corner of Main and Court Streets occupies the site of Nevada City's first city hall, known as the courthouse. Constructed soon after incorporation in the spring of 1851, it included a sturdy jail. A cemetery for paupers was located at the rear. Within a few months an ordinance was passed prohibiting more burials, but the area was called Potter's Hill for many years.

The only reminder of the town's first seat of government is the name of the steep little street running between Main and Coyote. (23)

# St. Canice's

Nevada City's first Catholic church opened on the corner of Washington and Coyote Streets in the spring of 1853. The present brick structure was built on the same lot in 1864. Father Griffin named it after a cathedral in Kilkenny, Ireland, his birthplace. (24)

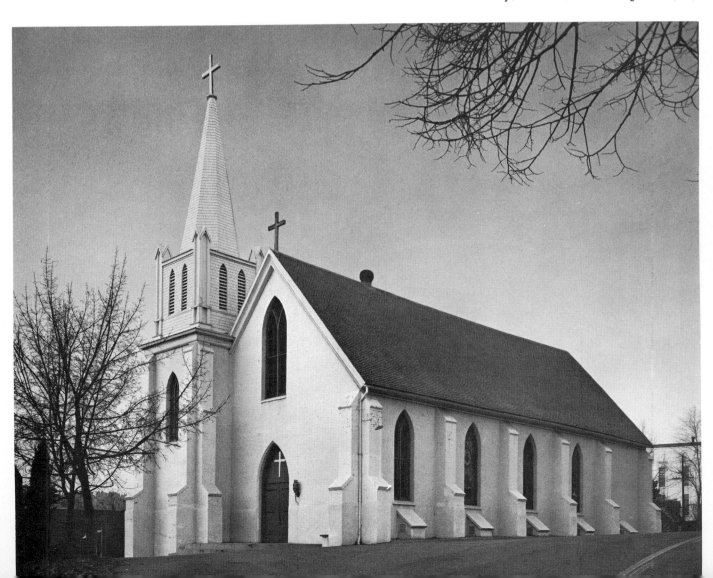

## Old Congregational

The old Congregational church, now Baptist, was built in 1864. The parsonage, called *Contentment* (left), was added in 1874. Final rites for Sutter's son were held in previous church, burned in 1863. (25)

## On Aristocracy Hill

Nevada Street runs down this broad eminence, which is more ridge than hill. Historic Gillet Nursery is nearby (gate at end of Nihell Street).

On the hill's upper reaches, maples flame in early October. Then the sun slants low through autumnal haze to warm a tracery of old ironwork. (26)

# By Buggy and Sleigh

Fresh from medical school in New York, Robert Menzo Hunt came to California by the Isthmus of Panama and tried mining and lumbering for two years. Turning to his profession he created a reputation for skill, warmth, generosity and strength of character that has endured through the years. Orphans, foreign immigrants, hospital patients and needy families had reason to remember him; it was said he never sent a bill unless you changed doctors.

Such a man had special meaning to a generation living in mountain isolation in an age innocent even of aspirin. Seeing patients often meant guiding his horse and buggy over muddy tracks in pitch blackness or driving his sleigh through an icy blizzard. Kerosene lamps gave him light, roaring fires in wood stoves heated water, and perhaps his best medicine was the devotion with which he served the afflicted and calmed those whose lives had brushed with fate.

Dr. Hunt built this stately home topped with a widow's walk in 1884, replacing an 1870 brick structure he had torn down because he believed the dampness in the bricks caused rheumatism. (27)

Spacious interior has opulent detail. Below, the parlor; above, a window cornice; at right, front hall stairway. (Private residence, closed to public.)

84

# Bourbon Lodge and the Aristocracy

In the winter of 1852-3 a group of young Southerners mined with the Coyote Company, probably near the head of Manzanita Ravine. Next summer they pooled their take to build a neat cottage on the crest of Manzanita Hill overlooking town. Its architecture had a southern colonial flavor and they named it Bourbon Lodge.

These genteel bachelors disliked associating with the rough miners in the town beneath them; the unwashed gentry in turn began to refer bitingly to Manzanita Hill as Aristocracy Hill, a name which remains to this day.

Additions to the house have changed it some, but it escaped all of Nevada City's fires and is one of its oldest buildings. In its bones are memories of long ago, when juleps were sipped on the veranda on hot summer evenings, when edifying poker games were played before a cozy fire on winter nights, and youth found adventure in a raw new land. (28)

# From Biscuit and Whiskey to Sermons

Here Nevada City had its beginnings. This Trinity Episcopal church occupies the site of Caldwell's Upper Store, which was the original name for the settlement that sprang up on the banks of Deer Creek. Caldwell put his trading post together of logs and canvas in October of 1849, when the early miners were casually picking up fortunes in gold along the creeks.

This classic structure, opened in 1873, replaced its predecessor established in 1863 and consumed in one of the town's occasional holocausts. (29)

# On Boulder Hill: Only the Best

Lured by the gold fields and urged by adventure, twenty-year-old Martin Luther Marsh arrived in Nevada City in 1851 after a journey from Ohio by the Nicaragua route. He worked as a carpenter, left to mine at Iowa Hill and try other ventures, and finally returned to enter the lumber business. His brother Dan joined him and they set up a sawmill on Little Deer Creek (the site is now Pioneer Park). The enterprise boomed, and in 1873 Martin built this magnificent home, using carefully seasoned sugar pine for the interior woodwork. There was no stinting materials or craftsmanship.

His wife died before its completion, and Marsh with the help of housekeepers raised his four children here. Marsh's granddaughter Lucille and her late husband James B. Christie restored the house to its former glory in 1955, utilizing many of the original furnishings.

The front yard is shaded by towering firs and cedars. Through their branches may be seen the multipaned cupola, a fashionable touch of the period. (30)

Above left, upstairs hallway and a bedroom. Above right, bowl and pitcher provided washing facilities in days of limited plumbing. At right, shaving stand is placed for best light softly filtering through old shutters. (Private residence, closed to public.)

# Along Park Avenue

Remembrance of things past, on the road to Pioneer Park. (31)

Restored elegance.

Cherry tree blooms anew beyond time-worn portico.

Distinctive ornamentation behind a wild garden.

Tributaries of Deer Creek were among the richest of nature's treasuries. During a brief moment in time, the fall of 1849, the deposits of centuries were pried out of crevices with pocket knives, and it was a poor miner who could not glean a pound of gold a day.

Then the easy pickings were gone, and Little Deer Creek was left much as it is today, tumbling over granite under the alders in Pioneer Park, an area once known as Pound Diggings. (32)

# A Pound of Gold
# a Day

91

# The Red Castle

Perched precariously on Prospect Hill is this dramatic brick house known as the Red Castle. Built in 1857 by Squire John Williams for his son Lorin, lawyer and mining man of promise, the Castle was the scene of many social gatherings. Young Williams, a member of the local band, enjoyed serenading townfolk on Sundays by tooting his cornet on the veranda, the vibrant notes floating over a citizenry going its churchly ways or recovering from the night before. (33)

# A Man of Action

Desperately ill with fever, young Bill Stewart jounced into the outskirts of Nevada City on a haywagon in 1850. At a spring on the banks of Deer Creek he lay down to die or get well, and finally recovered enough to make his way into town. He mined in Coyoteville while studying law, passed the bar in 1853, became county district attorney, later California attorney general, and devised many basic mining laws. On occasion he backed up courtroom presentations with his fists.

He built this home in 1855 and after two years sold it to Judge Niles Searls. Stewart moved to Downieville and in 1860 joined the silver rush to the Comstock, where he helped write the constitution for the new state of Nevada and became its first U. S. Senator. When the torrential downpours of December 1862 washed out his Virginia City mining venture, he crossed the stormy Sierra afoot and on horseback, rowed a boat over flood waters to Sacramento, caught a steamboat to San Francisco, borrowed money to rebuild, and returned the same way—all in nine days. By such feats did William Morris Stewart add a shining page to the chronicles of the West. (*Right: Nevada State Historical Society.*) (34)

93

Dark sign on top beam of tower is plate of bridge's maker, A. S. Hallidie & Co. Other sign gives notice of $25 fine for riding or driving across faster than a walk. A gas lamp hangs over roadway. (California Historical Society.)

Present Pine Street bridge supported from below by iron arch.

# From Here to the Cable Cars

Andrew S. Hallidie, inventor of San Francisco's famed cable cars, gained much of his wire rope experience in swinging a bridge across this canyon. He was 25 years old when in 1861 he contracted to put a suspension bridge over Deer Creek to replace a county structure damaged by flood and hard service.

Despite legal problems and bad weather the work was finished in May, 1862, at a cost of $9000. In July, the weight of two wagons heavily loaded with hay pulled loose a defective cable anchorage and two men and 15 oxen dropped into the gorge with the wagons and were killed.

Hallidie repaired the bridge, which served until 1904. He patented his wire rope suspension bridge in 1867 and went on to everlasting renown with his 1873 invention of the cable car. (35)

94

In later years the towers of Hallidie's bridge were enclosed for weather protection. (Elza Kilroy.)

This log structure occupies the site of an early crossing of Deer Creek at the foot of Bridge Street. Bill Stewart recovered from his illness near here.

View upstream from present bridge. The Red Castle stands high in the distance. Heavy summer foliage conceals Deer Creek and the secret fishermen's trails that follow its tumbling waters. Flowing in unseen from the right is Gold Run, down whose banks swept the restless tide of Argonauts pursuing westward visions of gold and adventure.

# Past and Future

In 1857 Nevada City was a raw but cohesive gold camp, already taking on all the attributes of a permanent community successfully serving the lives and habits of its citizens. During succeeding generations the plantings of the pioneers grew bountifully and the gracious homes and unique street patterns grouped around Deer Creek came to be recognized as giving the city a special unity and charm not found elsewhere in the gold country. Below is an artist's conception of the freeway now in progress. (*Above: Nevada City Public Library. Below: Doris Foley Collection.*)

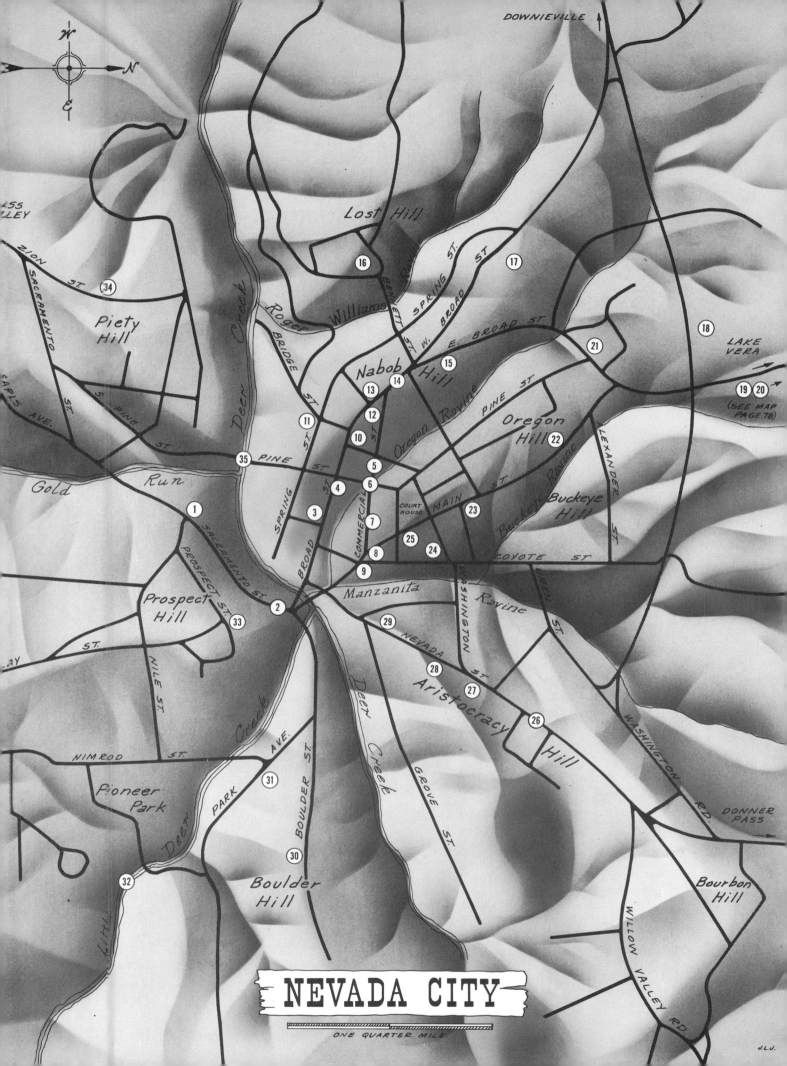

# NEVADA CITY

ONE QUARTER MILE